THE MALVERN HILLS AND WESTWARD

THE MALVERN HILLS AND WESTWARD

TRAVELS THROUGH THE MALVERNS AND EAST HEREFORDSHIRE

ARCHIE MILES

BEACON HILL HOUSE

For MF and JF, Cynthia and John, my Folks
with love and thanks

First published in Great Britain in 2002 by
Beacon Hill House
23 Worcester Road, Great Malvern, Worcs WR14 4QY.
Website: www.beaconbooksmalvern.co.uk

Designed by Carter Graphics, Worcester
Originated by Greenshires Group Ltd., Leicester

A CIP record for this book is available from the British Library

Papers used in the production of this book are natural, recyclable products made from wood grown in sustainable forests

ISBN 0-9542690-1-2 (Hb)
ISBN 0-9542690-0-4 (Pb)

Printed and bound in Singapore by Tien Wah Press Pte. Limited

Misty winter view east from Bromyard towards the Malvern Hills.

Double rainbow over
Stoke Lacy.

CONTENTS

Ewes and lambs
in a misty Wye
Valley morning.

Towering larches or a shot splintered sky?

AUTHOR'S ACKNOWLEDGEMENT

Archie would like to express his deep gratitude to Stuart and Anne-Marie Broadhurst, whose support made this book possible.

INTRODUCTION

A vivid memory still lingers with me, although some twelve years have elapsed since I climbed that hill. At 5.00 a.m., as an early summer sun broke upon the land from way back east, beyond Worcester plain and Cotswold scarp, I scaled the ancient ramparts of British Camp. Not a soul in sight. A light yet surprisingly chill breeze whipped the wiry upland grasses into submission. Daybreak's distinctive mellow sunlight stroked the hill tops, shunting outrageously steep Malvernesque shadows far into the undulating landscape of Herefordshire. I breasted the Camp summit and stood transfixed.

Sometimes the intensity of a natural wonder leaves me powerless to act for a while, caught between the need to make a picture from a brief if not fleeting glimpse of light and land perfectly aligned and the desire to simply soak up the whole magical experience. As the sun gradually began to warm my back, the shadow hills drew gently in to their casting parents, and a pair of early-rising buzzards wheeled lazily high above me, I began to make pictures.

From that day I knew that the land laid before me was somewhere special and somewhere I had to explore, but little realising the ultimate significance, for this was to be my future home.

When I first made acquaintance with the Malvern Hills and their environs it was to develop a photo essay on the landscape that inspired Sir Edward Elgar to write many of his finest works. I immersed myself in his music and delved into several of the biographies before embarking upon the legwork to seek out many of his special places. A voyage of discovery became my own personal inspiration.

The risk of living anywhere, no matter how remarkable or beautiful, is that before long whatever splendours surround one become over familiar and taken for granted. Herefordshire, and for that matter neighbouring Shropshire, can boast some of finest and most extensive tracts of unspoilt country landscape in England. Industry has never been over intrusive in these counties of principally agricultural economies; but even the agriculture has been of the non intensive type, providing a legacy of largely unchanged landscapes rich in biodiversity.

Ancient hedgerows abound. Woodlands supporting rich and varied flora and fauna; a few still ringing with the clamour of coppicers, green woodworkers or charcoal burners. Meadows untrammelled by pesticides and herbicides sporting vivid clouds of wild flowers. Old fashioned orchards with faltering rows of aged apple and perry pear trees, festooned with mistletoe. Narrow lanes lead this way and that between squat red sandstone churches and chocolate box black and white cottages.

The Malvern Hills seem to be a landmark from the flatlands to the east; a guardian gateway to the hidden treasure of Herefordshire. The town of Malvern still retains an air of Victorian gentility, nestling in the lee of the ancient hills. The supremely pure water which gushes forth from the hills above contains absolutely no mineral traces whatsoever, but it still brought spa status fame and fortune to the township and many of its nineteenth century entrepreneurs. The great and the good came from far and wide convinced that imbibing the water, indulging in the many water therapies on offer and taking bracing walks along the hills would do them the world of good.

On a fine day the view west from the Malvern Hills takes the eye some fifty miles to the far side of Herefordshire and the great sleeping beast of the Black Mountains with its distinctive slope of Hay Bluff dipping down at the northern end to the famous town of books, Hay on Wye. This book may only bestride half that vista, yet there is still much to explore and enjoy on the various highways and byways to the City of Hereford. A landscape of simple pleasures awaits, brim full of mysterious little lanes, hidden villages, cracking pubs, and views to die for.

Heading further north from the northern reaches of the Malvern range slip through shady lanes around the villages of Alfrick and Suckley, occasionally spotting old orchards or hop gardens – once the mainstay of the local agriculture, but now drastically reduced in number, before dipping down into the Teme Valley at Knightwick. Here, in the springtime, begins a riot of cherry blossom in long neglected orchards, as well as great drifts of pure white damson blossom lining many an old hedgerow.

Westward, across the humps and bumps of Bringsty Common, before a required diversion to marvel at the splendid medieval moated farmhouse at Lower Brockhampton. Hard by, the little market town of Bromyard seems to have changed little over recent years. The butcher, the baker and the candle stick maker all ply their trades in preference to the plethora of olde tea shoppes and knick-knack emporiums. Very refreshing to find unpretentious shops selling stuff that the local folks need.

North-west of Bromyard lies one of the most sparsely populated quarters of Herefordshire, where the diligent explorer will discover remnants of the Beeching clobbered Worcester to Leominster railway line, a little known but impressive Iron Age hillfort at Wall Hills or simply delicious little hamlet names like the group including Stoke Bliss, Sweet Green and Pie Corner.

To the large market town of Leominster wedged firmly in the fork of the rivers Arrow and Lugg. At first sight the name might seem to suggest the presence of lions – unlikely! Apparently the first part of the name is derived from an old Welsh word for 'streams', whilst the medieval Latin *leonis* means 'of the marshes'. Today Leominster may be bypassed by the frantic roar of the A49, but it is still a vibrant community. Architecturally it's a mixed bag. The jewel is undoubtedly John Abel's black and white Grange Court, built in 1633, just a stroll around the Green from The Priory, a conjunction of periods and styles, but still boasting some remarkable mid-twelfth century carving of the Hereford School around its west door. Some handsome Georgian architecture leads down to the commercial hub of the town, where fine old timber-framed buildings stand cheek by jowl with lesser inspired frontages of the latter twentieth century.

The main arterial route of the A49 strikes the western boundary for this book and shortly after passing the chocolate sweet smell of the Cadbury factory at Marlbrook it snakes over Dinmore Hill past the Queenswood Country Park with its beautiful arboretum and woodland walks, before racing across the flatlands west of the River Lugg into the city of Hereford.

Hereford's centrepiece must be its cathedral. Rebuilding began in the early twelfth century, shortly after the whole town was sacked by marauding Welshmen (it's probably just as well that Hereford United no longer play Cardiff City these days!). An abundance of chevron ornament and the interlace carving typical of the Hereford School adorns the Norman nave. The most famous treasure of the cathedral is the *Mappa Mundi*, which now has its very own shrine; drawn by Richard of Haldingham, a prebend of the cathedral, way back in 1290 on a single cow hide, it depicts the world as he knew it along theological lines. A collection of ancient books and manuscripts also rest in chains, shackled to Jacobean bookcases in the library. The view from the tower, accessed on one of the frequent open days, is a cracking all round view of the city. The broad sweep of the River Wye flows a stone's throw from the cathedral, beneath the six spans of the Old Bridge, which is actually the oldest bridge across the whole course of the Wye, dating back to about 1490. Floods have come and gone on a regular basis, but still the old stones sit resolute. Architectural heritage is rich and diverse in the city; whether it be the timber-framed museum piece of The Old House set in slightly incongruous isolation amid High Town's bustling shops, the Gothic menagerie of beasts running rampant across the Library and Museum building in Broad Street, or even the imposing red sandstone railway station which has welcomed visitors since 1855. Attention to detail will detain the architecturophile long in this city. Hereford was once home to several major cider producers, but now the Bulmers empire holds sway, and for a month or two in the autumn the sweet lip-smacking aroma of apple pies wafts across the city. Well, of course it isn't really pies, merely part of the pasteurization process prior to cider making. The livestock market still takes place every Wednesday bringing country folks into the city from far and wide, and is accompanied by a loud and colourful open market close by. Cultural events frequently revolve around the one of the city's most recent constructions – The Courtyard – a great new venue providing theatre, film, concerts and gallery space.

The course of the Wye meanders southward from Hereford through a broad valley of fertile farmland, being joined by the Lugg at Mordiford. Gradually, the river valley narrows as the serpentine meanders carve steep cliffs round their outer bends, usually clad in dense woodland. This is a grand stretch of river to launch a canoe and drift gently downstream keeping a weather eye for herons, cormorants, swans and the iridescent blue flash of darting kingfishers. The Wye is also a Mecca for fishermen, seeking that record salmon, but there's plenty of room for everyone.

The soaring spire of St. Mary's church, clearly discernable for miles around on its hill top perch, announces the old market town of Ross-on-Wye set in picturesque splendour above a broad bend in the river. Like so many Herefordshire towns the the prevailing materials for the older buildings are black and white timber-framed construction or the local red sandstone. The town centre forms a triangle about the fine old arcaded Market House, which still hosts a weekly market.

North once more, but this time striking east of the Wye, and the dominant landscape feature is the Woolhope Dome. Nothing to do with Millennium debacles, but a wonderful natural oasis, featuring a complex geology, some of Herefordshire's most remarkable ancient woodland and a fascinating network of ancient paths and lanes set about with unspoilt hamlets and farmsteads. Indeed, this is the northern extremity of the Wye Valley AONB. From Marcle Ridge there is a breathtaking view across the gentle undulations of the Leadon valley to the town of Ledbury and the distant Malvern Hills beyond.

Much Marcle affords the visitor much joy. St. Bartholomew's church houses some fine monuments, but set close by is one of the most spectacular ancient yew trees in Britain. Hollow, as all these ancient churchyard sentinels tend to be, this tree has a girth of some thirty feet and could well be as old as 3,000 years. This obviously predates the church, or even the arrival of Christianity. There is a current belief that these trees had a religious significance to pre-Christian cultures, thus it could be surmised that this endures as a monument to the conjunction of ancient or pagan faith with the 'new way' of Christ. A little way across the fields from the church lies Hellens, begun in 1292 for the de Helyon family, it is still owned by their direct descendants, and presents a virtual time capsule of the seventeenth century and beyond. Famous visitors include the Black Prince and "Bloody" Mary Tudor, but one of the house's most bloodthirsty moments occurred during the Civil War, when Roundheads burst in and slaughtered the family priest. His ghost reputedly haunts the house. If all this is too exhausting repair to the cider works of Henry Weston & Sons and sample some of the delicious ciders and perries on offer.

Supplying the needs of the residents of south-east Herefordshire is the busy little town of Ledbury. Again, some splendid black and white buildings take the eye, and none more so than the Market Hall. Completed in 1655 it was reputedly built by John Abel and, unusually, it stands upon pillars of sweet chestnut rather than the more common place oak. Around the corner, the photographer's dream – Church Lane, a medieval showpiece of jettied timber-framed buildings which overhang the cobbled path to St. Michael's church.

Leaving Ledbury climb over the hill and take a detour to explore one of Herefordshire's grandest residences at Eastnor Castle. Built in 1812 to designs by Sir Robert Smirke (also responsible for Covent Garden and the British Museum) it is a blend of neo-Norman and Italianate which gives the impression of a traditional child's toy fort with its huge round corner turrets. The castle is still very much a home and contains many sumptuous rooms and family treasures, while outside a deer park stretches away to the Malvern Hills, and that Iron Age bastion of British Camp once again commands the view.

In a world which appears to drive increasingly frantically towards who-knows-what it's an enduring pleasure and comfort to find a corner where the pace of life steps down a gear or two, the stars twinkle in a clear night sky, and the air is clean. I want to be in touch with the earth, watch the seasons sweep across familiar views, catch the sounds of foraging badgers or the unearthly screams of mating foxes in the night, smell honeyed apple blossom in the spring and the bitter scent of the hop harvest in the autumn. Having discovered this place I want to stay as long as I can.

Hoar frosted cider apples.

Rich autumn hues along the Malvern Hills towards Worcestershire Beacon. The ridge top path setting the boundary between Herefordshire and Worcestershire.

ON THE HILLS

I've sat here many's the time,
Stared far to each compass point
As I straddled the back of the beast,
Who lay with his rump to the sun.

North stood the beacon of Worcester,
The beast head brow skimmed oft close
By passing clouds
And Welsh winds

South lay the beacon of Hereford,
Camp ramparts folded and tiered.
Bold Britons' faught.
Heroes long gone.

East stretched the plain, on past Severn,
Into haze, cloud or Cotswold plateau.
Crosshatch landscape,
Pierced by spires.

West held the secrets in every hill fold;
A half-timbered, tree speckled, sleepy land,
Where people had time
To stop and stare.

The northern part of the Malvern Hills stretches away from the lower ramparts of Herefordshire Beacon.

Drifting high above British Camp on a late summer's evening, the lilliputian figures waving and calling from the summit sound deceptively close.

Evening sunlight illuminates British Camp, one of the finest Iron Age hillforts in Britain.

A Morgan motor car sweeps down Jubilee Drive with Worcestershire Beacon in the distance.

Autumnal view south along the Malvern Hills from the summit of Worcestershire Beacon; the distinctive profile of British Camp in the distance.

Golden fronds of larch and silvery whisps of rosebay willowherb adorn the western slopes of the Malverns above Colwall.

A light dusting of snow picks
out the contours of North Hill.

A cosy hollow in the
western slopes of the
Malvern Hills, above
West Malvern, and a
tempting view far out
across Herefordshire.

The town of
Great Malvern,
tucked beneath the
protective Hills,
and the glorious
patchwork of the
Worcestershire
plain beyond.

Terra cotta terrifying
dragon scrambles
across a roof at the
end of Graham Road.

Three details of Victorian utility and
decoration in Great Malvern.

FOR A MOMENT
IN MALVERN

On a hill above pure water
A dolphin waits to dive.
Sun come up, gas glow fades,
Malvern comes alive.

Small boy with a big stick
Clatters down the rails,
And makes the lilies quiver;
Griffins twitch their tails.

Rainbow shafts come creeping
Over polished marble floors,
While the unicorn sits smiling,
And the lion waves his paws.

Don't let the dragon scare you,
Belle Vue is fair to see;
Then bluebirds call you over
For another cup of tea.

Although established during the eleventh century, the splendid edifice of Malvern Priory, viewed here from Priory Park, is essentially a fifteenth century building. Treasures within include medieval stained glass, floor tiles and delightful carvings on the misericords.

Dramatic view of the Abbey Gateway. Something of a misnomer, since the Priory never achieved the status of an abbey, a more appropriate name might be Priory Gatehouse. Even so, today it does form one of the gateways to the imposing Abbey Hotel.

Griffin gargoyles perch
atop the Council House
in Priory Park.

Just a small sample
of the glorious
painted and stained
glass, incorporated
in the Council House
reconstruction of
the 1870's.

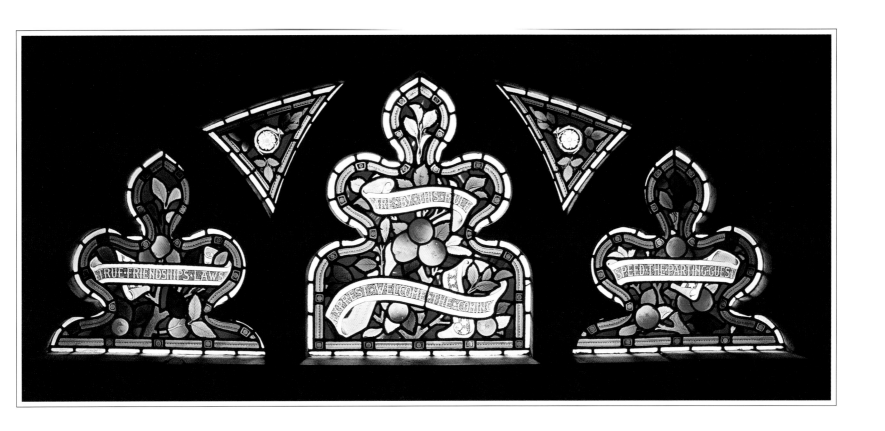

TRUE·FRIENDSHIPS·LAWS

SPEED·THE·PARTING·GUEST

33

A superbly restored 1937 Morgan Super Sports 3-wheeler. Although they may now favour four wheels instead of three, as the company fast approaches its centenary, the internationally renowned Morgan sports cars are still very much hand built in Malvern.

CHO 183

The clear pure waters emanating from beneath the Malvern Hills contain absolutely no mineral content whatsoever, and yet Victorian high society flocked to Malvern to take 'The Cure'. Holy Well is but one of numerous points around the Hills where the water may be taken, and has barely changed since the nineteenth century.

The undulating Malvern range viewed from hills above Cradley

The cultivation of hops has declined in recent years, and much of those still grown are new dwarf varieties carried on shorter hop poles and thus more easily harvested by specialised machines. Here and there hops may be found growing wild around old farmyards or in hedges, where they might last have been grown decades ago. Hop kilns, known as oast houses to Kentish folk, still define the the old hop growing farms, although many have now been converted to private dwellings. Once savoured, the pungent smell of harvested hops is never forgotten.

Wintery view south from Westfield, near Cradley.

THREE HORSES

Three black horses stood stock still,
Frozen in a fraction on a snowclad hill.

Scrawled on the blank of an artist's pad;
Do they run to the call of a farmer's lad?

Have they names like Sooty or Blackie or Sweep?
Is it true that horses must stand up to sleep?

Will they get cold? Are they happy or sad?
Does the same field get boring, driving them mad?

If it snows in the night do they still stand forlorn,
Become dappled grey then white in the storm?

When morning comes may they have disappeared?
Snopaqued from the picture as may have been feared.

Three white horses stood stock still,
Hidden in the image of a snowclad hill.

In a long neglected cherry
orchard above the Teme Valley
at Darby's Green.

Winter floods in
the Teme Valley
near Doddenham.

Hazy early morning sunshine creeps over a farmstead at Horsham in the Teme Valley.

The twelfth century church of St. Andrew at Shelsley Walsh contains one of the finest Perpendicular chancel screens to be found in the area.
A detail is illuminated briefly through one of the stained glass windows.

The Visitors! A startling little homestead hidden away on Bringsty Common.

Inquisitive Hereford cattle near Knightwick.

A typical landscape feature of north Herefordshire are the great snow drifts of damson blossom in late March or early April. Traditionally it was common practise to plant these trees in hedgerows around orchards, where they provided a protective windbreak, an early lure to bring pollinating bees to the orchard, and a source of fruit. Until the middle of last century train loads of damsons were sent to the Lancashire cotton industry for their dying properties. Today they are a great resource for local wine and jam makers.

Details of the pure white blossom, the deep purple fruits and the resinous sap which often seeps from cuts or abrasions in the boughs. Country folk often used to chew this as a kind of natural chewing gum.

Late summer sun across
Bringsty Common with the
distant Malvern Hills beyond.

A similar view, but
on a misty late
autumnal morning.

The graceful silver birch finds plenty of space to colonize on Bringsty Common.

Beautiful but dangerous, the bold red caps of fly agaric stand out among the leaf litter beneath birches.

One of the most splendid
specimens of fern-leaved beech
in Britain is to be found in the
gardens of Kyre Park.

The impressive
eighteenth century façade
of Kyre Park overlooks
gardens and parkland
thought to have been the
work of the famous
Capability Brown.

Not to be missed - the superb medieval moated manor house at Lower Brockhampton, complete with its own little gatehouse, and now in the ownership of the National Trust.

Autumn leaves in a lake on the Brockhampton Estate.

View from Warren Wood on top of Bromyard Downs, with the town below on the far side of the Frome Valley.

The reverse view. Late afternoon up Broad Street, Bromyard, with the Downs in the distance.

56

A fine oak tree in
winter and summer.

OAK

Oh Herefordshire weed
Thou art an oak.
Fear not,
For no right thinking person
Will pluck you disdainful
From this garden.

Oh Herefordshire weed
Thou art....another oak.
Sprung from a burial
Jay thieved acorn;
Held fast in a hedge,
Dodged by the plough.

Oh Herefordshire weed
Thou art..........yet another oak.
In mid life vigour displayed,
Houses and ships you hold;
Home to a multitude.
You reap respect.

Oh Herefordshire weed
Just an oak.
Your stag-headed boughs
Proclaim numbered days.
Hollow bole;
Home for an owl.

Oh Herefordshire weed
Once an oak.
You are falling back
To the earth that made you.
Your grain lingers long;
Carved, planed and sawn.

Oh Herefordshire weed
A waiting oak.
In burrows far and wide
Acorn sleeps lightly
Awaits the call
Of sun and moon.

A distant deluge pours
from an impressive anvil
cloud over Little Cowarne.

Harebells on
Bromyard Downs.

Autumn and winter views
east from Bromyard,
across the Frome Valley
to the distant Malvern Hills.

Lovingly restored to its prime, the old railway station at Rowden Mill is now a private house, but this is how it must have looked before the demise of the Worcester - Leominster line under the axe of the infamous Dr. Beeching in the 1960's.

Early spring in the sparsely populated countryside around Thornbury.

Old fashioned farmhouse orchard at Stoke Lacy. The dappled shade and heady honeyed scent of blossom make these places particularly special in the month of May. This orchard, typically, contains a mixture of dessert, culinary and cider apples originally planted to serve every need of the family. Moreover this orchard is a habitat oasis, containing ancient greensward, wild flowers, suitable trees and bordering hedges to encourage a variety of birdlife, and refuge for badgers and foxes.

The delicate blossoms of crab apple. Before the advent of the redoubtable Malling and Merton rootstocks most selected varieties were grafted on to crabstocks. The trees were also frequently planted for pollination purposes and the fruits make an excellent country wine.

Cider press sculpture in
Brockhampton Woods,
by Barry Mason.

Many different types of apple all from one orchard. Extremely old and virtually forgotten varieties still exist in many Herefordshire orchards, and fortunately a few enthusiasts are rediscovering these and grafting new trees.

Hoar frosted orchard at Stoke Lacy.

OUR ORCHARD

You gave me the sign that life would renew
When your soft leaves of spring began to burst through.

When the moles had all done with their tunnelling spree,
And the fieldfares had flown far over the sea.

You poured forth your blossom of pink and of white,
While the collared doves cooed in a hole out of sight,

In a tree that was hollow but still threw its flush,
I heard an owl scream in the night's velvet hush.

You set out your wares of pear, apple and plum,
Ripened and sweetened 'neath hot summer sun.

As the days drew back and the fruit dropped free
With baskets and ladders we stripped each tree.

Soon pies were full filled and cider was pressed,
And the fair harvest table welcomed each guest,

Where we all sat around and remembered the year,
With the joy that you brought us by just being here.

Leominster Morris wassail an old orchard. Traditionally performed on Twelfth Night (the old New Year) the custom was once widespread throughout the western counties of England. Derived from pagan beliefs, by the use of song, dance, fire, libations of cider, and a great deal of noise the idea was to awaken the benevolent tree spirits who guarded the orchard, and thus secure a fine harvest.

The tiny isolated church of St.Andrew at Leysters.

The Romans reputedly
planted vineyards in the
region, but only in recent
years has there been an
upsurge in the cultivation of
vines and the production of
some fine and distinctive
wines. These are
Reichensteiner grapes which
seem particularly suited to
Herefordshire soils.

The grape harvest is very
much a manual affair as
shown by this lass in her
Marigolds, at Broadfield
Court, Bodenham.

Traditional hedge laying is slowly but surely having something of a resurgence, and the winter months find several such craftsmen with plenty of work across the county.

Pollarded willows by the river at Moreton on Lugg.

Voluptuous carving of Eve, by John Abel, to be found on Grange Court.

Grange Court, Leominster, is one of the most important buildings in Herefordshire, and boasts something of a chequered history. Originally built in 1633, by the renowned John Abel (the King's Carpenter), the building was originally sited in the middle of the town as the Market Hall, and would have been open arched on the ground floor. In 1855 it was dismantled and promptly bought for the princely sum of £95 by one Francis Davis. Shortly afterwards it was then sold on for the same figure to the local M.P. John Arkwright. He offered it to the local council if they would undertake its reconstruction. They declined, and the building lay in pieces in a builder's yard until Arkwright later rebuilt it as his family home on its present site. In the 1930s there was the threat of it being sold and exported to America, but luckily the local council stepped in, paying £3,000 for it, and brought it back into civic use.

A grotesque character carved
on one of the capitals inside the
twelfth century doorway to
Leominster Priory. The stylised
tendrils emanating from the
face, redolent of the Green Man,
would appear to be brambles.

At Queenswood
arboretum on top
of Dinmore Hill an
Acer palmatum in
autumnal glory.

The Old House in Hereford's
High Town is an ancient
survivor in the midst of a
modern city. Now standing in
splendid isolation it was once
part of a group of buildings
erected in 1621 and known as
Butcher's Row. A variety of
merchants, including saddlers,
ironmongers, fish-mongers and
a bank, owned the premises
through the nineteenth and
early twentieth centuries,
before Lloyds presented the
building to the city in 1928.
It now contains a museum of
life in the Civil War period.

Hereford Cathedral
glimpsed across the
river Wye.

Victoria footbridge - an elegant pedestrian crossing of the Wye, links the city to Bishop's Meadows.

Commissioned by
Herefordshire Council as
part of the City Carving
Scheme, 'The Mundi Tree'
by Emma Richards-Ward is
but one of a citywide
collection of diverse and
fascinating sculptures.
Carved on a life expired
tree in Bishop's Meadows it
features the cathedral, the
new and old bridges across
the Wye, as well as the
Mundi Tree itself.

Hereford Cathedral
viewed across The Close
in the early morning.

Hidden away in the cloisters are a few interesting blocks of stone, one of which bears this haunting representation of the Green Man. Removed during one of the periods of restoration of the cathedral many years ago it is uncertain as to where he was originally sited. Almost certainly of medieval origin it seems highly appropriate that in the realm of the oak he has oak leaves issuing from his mouth.

Exhibited in the Cider
Museum is this collection
of costrels, little barrels
which were once used to
take cider out into the
fields for the farm
labourers, and beakers
made from cow horns.

The Cowarne Red

In 1811 Thomas Andrew Knight of Downton published his *Pomona Herefordiensis*. Something of a mover and shaker in his time as a producer of new varieties of fruit and vegetables, he was elected as the president of the London Horticultural Society in the same year. Available only as a subscription partwork this particular plate depicts the Cowarne Red. The freshness of this hand coloured plate after almost two hundred years is truly remarkable, as is the style of the specimen complete with blemished apples, insect nibbled leaves and attached lichen.

Creatures in Hereford -
playful monkeys scramble
across the Victorian
facade of the library
and museum in Broad
Street, whilst Walenty
Pytel's fish swim back and
forth along a balustrade
on the recently opened
Left Bank Village.

HEREFORD TILES

Roundels and squiggles and lions and fish,
Fleur-de-lis and griffin profiles
Have all been caught in the shape of a square,
To be found on Hereford Tiles.

On library stair or emporium floor;
In a station or old civic hall;
You'll find Hereford Tiles all round the town
In a porch, round a fire, on a wall.

Thousands were made in Victoria's reign,
For cathedrals and churches worldwide.
Paving the way for the faithful to pray,
Bearing bishop or baby or bride.

Their colours endure a century's wear,
Their glazes set them apart.
The magical beauty of Hereford Tiles,
Each one a true work of art.

Victorian tiles from Godwin's Hereford Tile Works. William and Henry Godwin began making encaustic tiles at Lugwardine in 1852, adding a larger factory at Withington in 1863 to meet increasing demand. During their Victorian heyday these tiles were exported all over the world and incorporated in all manner of ecclesiastical and public buildings. The keen observer may still spy many of them worked into the decorative facades, porches and hallways of many of Hereford's buildings both public and private.

A bungalow in suburban Hereford claims its own few days of celebratory adornment with the flowering of its two splendid magnolias.

A gentle pace of life prevails on Castle Green.

Mistletoe is a plant which seems to do rather well in the clean air of Herefordshire, and although most commonly associated with old orchards it finds purchase on many other tree hosts; usually hawthorn, willow or common lime. However, this riverside tree bedecked in numerous clumps is a hybrid black poplar.

Dinedor Camp just to the south of Hereford is an Iron Age hillfort, which affords outstanding views of the city, and also contains some impressive trees, such as these mighty beeches.

Remnant of a remarkable perry pear tree in the water meadows near Holme Lacy. In 1790 this tree was documented as covering 3/4 of an acre. The secondary trunks were, and still are, formed by branches falling and layering.

Perry pears, the small bitter fruits used to make the delicious drink of perry, against the distinctive tessellated bark pattern of the pear tree.

View north across
the Wye Valley
towards King's
Caple from Sellack.

View east
along the Wye at
Ballingham Hill.

Eighteenth
century gravestones
at the church of
St. Dubricius,
Hentland.

It could have been anywhere;
A lane end somewhere.
Mournful hinges wail,
Seized fast in lonesome repose,
But admit one more.
One who stumbles amidst the stones,
Whilst in memoriam in its own way
Stumbles half crazed,
Reeling and lolling
Slabs,
Wild amongst a wilderness
Of tangled herbs and
Bitter starved grasses.

Dearly beloved.
Sadly forgotten.
The elements peel away the lives,
Recalled once in fine hewn face;
Far grander in final repose,
Their each special span seems now
Ancient fascinating normality.

As each stone took lodging here
Each mason found fit
To carve a guardian angel
To watch over the gone,
And stare at the going.
Faces have cracked and flaked,
Taken lichen and moss to their cheek.

Above or below the sod little changes,
Yet change will continue for eternity.

Two views of the unusual St. Catherine's church at Hoarwithy. Designed by J.P. Seddon, the building was actually a reworking and beautification process to improve a rather mundane existing structure. Work began in 1854 and took an amazing thirty years to complete, but the result is a triumph. A Romanesque campanile towering out of the Herefordshire countryside might seem bizarre, but it does work, and the interior is yet another treasure of artistry and craftsmanship.

104

View down the river towards
Ross-on-Wye late on an October
afternoon, the soaring spire of
St. Mary's church and the
Royal Hotel taking centre stage.

Market day in and
around the old Market
Hall in the centre of
Ross-on-Wye.

Alms houses, built in 1575,
on the road up to St. Mary's.

Mediterranean colours
come to Ross; guest
houses in Wye Street.

These two views of the
ancient yew tree at Linton
show how the same subject
changes with the effect of
different lighting only twenty
minutes apart. With a girth
of 33' this tree has been
estimated to be about 4,000
years old. Tragically, since
these pictures were taken,
the tree was inexplicably
striken by fire. Although the
hollow interior is now
charred, and some boughs
were damaged, this tough old
stager is still alive and
making every effort to renew.

A bend in the Wye
near How Caple.

Large-leaved lime is
one of Britain's rarest
broadleaf trees, yet the
Wye Valley supports
many fine specimens.
This great old tree on the
river bank below Capler
was clearly pollarded
many years ago.

Mistletoe at Mordiford.
In a flooded orchard
beside the river an old
apple tree is quite
infested by mistletoe.
The plant is a semi-
parasite and whilst it
draws sustainance from
the tree it will not harm
it. It's only the sheer
weight of great volumes
of the plant which may
eventually break boughs.

Club Day for The Heart of Oak Society at Fownhope falls on or around May 29th (Oak Apple Day) each year. This is a friendly society founded in 1876, with the aim of helping those less fortunate in the community through the levying of a small annual subscription. Initially the members process to the church for a service, afterwhich there is a walk around the village where hospitality (beer) is offered to all, before a grand lunch at The Green Man.

All Saints, Brockhampton, is a somewhat unusual church built in 1901-02 by William Lethaby in the Arts and Crafts style. From the outside it presents a somewhat beguiling combination of elements. The south doorway with its lapboard tower looks as if it were added on as an afterthought, but the thatched roof which should have been more comfortable on house or barn works surprisingly well. Inside the setting is simple, with one of the main themes being wild flowers, carved on the stalls of the chancel, embroidered on the altarcloth, hymn book covers and kneelers. There is much charm in the naivity and originality of such a church building, which represents a bold departure by all those responsible a century ago.

Shard mask of oak collected from the woodland floor in Haugh Wood.

Silvery stems of oak
coppice in Haugh Wood
in early spring.

Many compartments
of Haugh Wood are
given over to
commercial conifer
plantations, but
winter snows bring a
certain magic even to
these parts.

A stand of young beech trees burst into leaf in Haugh Wood. Although much of the wood is given over to commercial forestry its origins are many centuries old, and through its excellent network of paths and tracks their are many exciting discoveries to be made.

Heavy horse logger. Doug Joiner with 'Ella' at work in Childer Wood. This traditional form of timber extraction has proven conservation benefits for the woodland floor, being far less damaging than modern forestry machinery.

Wild cherry in flower
in a gully in Lea &
Paget's Wood above
Fownhope. This is one
of Herefordshire Nature
Trust's finest woodlands.

View across Lower
Buckenhill from Capler
Camp, with the Malvern
Hills in the distance.

120

Late summer on the
Woolhope Dome; the
view from Woolhope
towards Marcle Hill.

View east across
the Leadon Valley
from Marcle Ridge
towards Ledbury
and The Malverns.

Four of the many beautiful
wild flowers to be found in the
woodlands of the Woolhope
Dome, clockwise from left:
Common spotted orchid,
Stinking iris, Foxglove and
the scarce Herb-paris.

Early morning sunshine backlights wild daffodils.

Glorious spread of wild
daffodils in pastures at
Woolhope Cockshoot.
In amongst these
daffodils were wood
anemones - an indicator
species of ancient
woodland. Clearly
this land was once
continuous woodland
which was cleared a
long time ago.

DAFFODILS AT DAWN

Ice blue sky
Still clawed by leaflorn
Springtime waiting
Oak, ash and thorn.

Dew gems glint
Clear crystal bright beads;
Myriad mirrors
Fade to fluffy white seeds.

Puddles of gold
Splash meadows and rills,
As first burst
Morn sunshine slips over the hills.

Lost are the glades
Where sweet trumpets were born,
Still valley sweep
Cradles daffodils at dawn.

A Gloucester Old Spot pig forages for apples with a couple of friendly chickens at Woodredding Farm on Perrystone Hill.

Still open for business, but no longer in the ownership of Westons, the Garage at Much Marcle.

The main gateway into Hellens, at Much Marcle, a family house whose roots can be traced back to 1292, although most of the building in evidence today is essentially seventeenth century.

A splendid seventeenth century embroidered bedspread in the Cordova Room at Hellens.

The little banqueting hall or Courtroom at Hellens. The huge fireplace bears the crest of the Black Prince (1330-76), eldest son of Edward III. It is thought that this was a tribute to the Prince by his great friend James Audley, who was the tenant of Hellens in the mid fourteenth century.

Perry pear trees line the drive from Much Marcle village to Hellens. The avenue was reputedly planted in 1702 to commemorate the accession of Queen Anne, so it is doubtful whether any of the original trees still survive.

A mid thirteenth century Green Man on a capital in St. Bartholomew's church, Much Marcle.

Interior of the ancient yew tree at Much Marcle church. This one is 30' in girth, so only about 3,000 years old! It's interesting to ponder upon how many people have sat inside this tree, and for how many years.

Strawberry and vanilla - red and white hawthorn blossom surrounds this view eastward from Little Marcle.

Wild daffodils in Dymock Wood, a stone's throw from the Herefordshire border. Although many of these cheerful little flowers must have been lost to agricultural improvement and looting gardeners over the years it is still possible to see not only woods full of these flowers, but also meadows and the virges of the lanes around Dymock and Kempley.

The Trumpet Ploughing Match is held annually at the beginning of October, and attracts one of the largest entries of horse teams in Britain. Ploughmen (and women) come from as far afield as Scotland, the West Country and the Isle of Wight to compete. Even if the technicalities of ploughing the best furrow are a mystery to the layman it's still a totally absorbing experience watching man and beast working in close harmony.

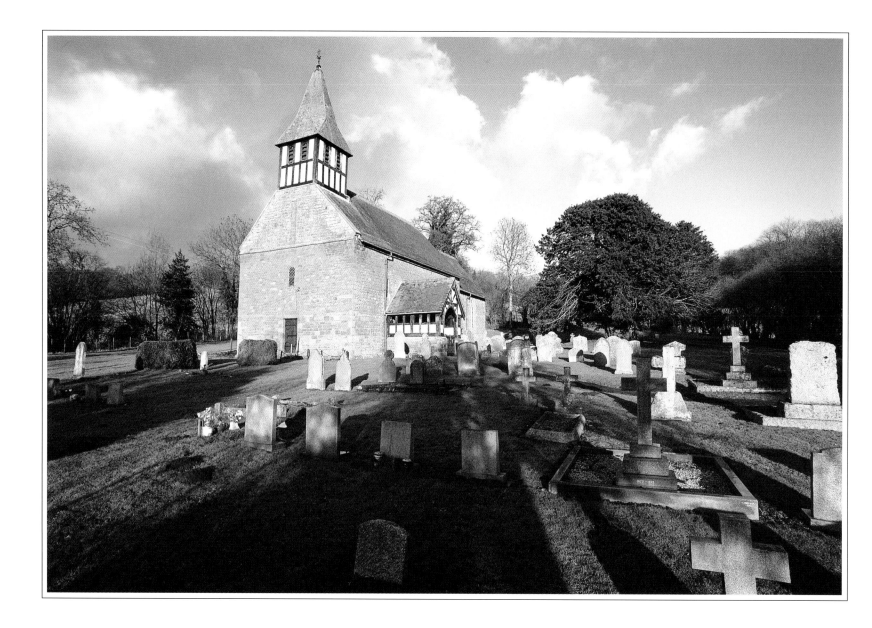

St. Michael's church at Castle Frome is a fairly unassuming little building with a quaint black and white timber framed belltower, but inside lies one of the masterpieces of the Hereford School of Norman sculpture. The main feature of the font is a depiction of the baptism of Christ by John the Baptist, including the hand of God and the dove of the Holy Spirit descending from above. An amusing touch are the fishes nibbling at Christ's feet.

Church Cottage and St. Lawrence's church, Stretton Grandison, and a cedar whose eventual size was probably not bargained for by the planter. The setting and the spire is reminiscent of those Christmas cards with toppered gents and crinolined ladies.

Seen from afar this field across the way from the church appeared to contain a crop of lavender. Closer inspection revealed it to be sage, and several acres of it!

143

Frosty morning on Stanley Hill, with the Malvern Hills in the distance.

STANLEY HILL'S COLD

Stanley Hill's cold, well he's stamping his feet,
And he's hugging his shoulders and rubbing his seat.
He's got three pair of socks and a daft bobble hat,
And a bright pink scarf from his cousin called Pat.
His boots are all furry and his trousers are lined
With some high tech fabric with cotton entwined.
He's got a big Arran jumper his gran had to knit,
But it's three sizes too large and it doesn't quite fit
Beneath the double quilt jacket with fur lined hood.
He's just stripped off and he feels quite good.

With a jolt and a start he wakes up in his bed;
Stanley Hill's sweating, it's all in his head.

Early morning aerial
view across the town
of Ledbury.

Ledbury
viewed from
Coneygree Wood.

An avenue of Common limes lead to St.John's church at Eastnor.

This beautiful thatched cottage at Eastnor has become rather famous and must surely by now have featured on a chocolate box.

The soft light of early
morning bathes the
toy fort turrets of
Eastnor Castle.

One of the most
amazing rooms in
Eastnor Castle is
the Gothic drawing
room designed by
Augustus Pugin.

151

Bitter winter day on the eastern slopes of British Camp.

Early sunlight and morning mists over the view southward from British Camp.

Autumnal view west
from Midsummer Hill
to the obelisk.

An intoxicating
carpet of bluebells
adorn the woodland
floor on the slopes
of Midsummer Hill.

Oil seed rape stretches away to a windbreak of poplars below Kilbury Camp.

Tempestuous clouds threaten, but the odd burst of sunlight manages to flood the landscape.

INDEX